DETOURS

DETOURS

DANIEL BOLAND

STONE FLOWER PRESS, OTTAWA

Stone Flower Press, Ottawa

Cover Photo: Angela Boland

Production Design: Jen Hamilton
Printed by: CreateSpace

Library and Archives Canada Cataloguing in Publication

Boland, Daniel, 1963–, author
        Detours / Daniel Boland.

Poems.
ISBN 978-0-9919073-3-5 (pbk.)

        I. Title.

PS8603.O45D48 2014   C811'.6   C2014-906083-1

ACKNOWLEDGEMENTS

Some of these poems have appeared in *Arborealis, Bywords, The Prairie Journal of Canadian Literature, The Saranac Review (U.S.A.)* and *The Trumpeter*. Two of the poems are forthcoming in the anthology *The Heart is Improvisational* (Guernica Editions). I wish to thank Tom Henighan for his ongoing support and his long-standing commitment to my writing. I would also like to thank Henry Beissel for his support.

For Rosie and Angela

TABLE OF CONTENTS

IF

DETOURS

I   IF

MIGRATION OF THE MONARCH

A September flight of butterflies—
unsteady, quavering
yet relentless in their goal.

They are tiny flags of independence unfurled in brilliant unison
or perhaps the silk
some ancient king might have worn.

They are a field of airborne oriental poppies
now on their way
to join some unfathomably
intricate tapestry.

A huge release
of new souls.

WATER DAMAGE

The yarrow has outdone itself this year—
needs some pruning, some tough love
to set it right
to yellow it up again.

And then water, of course.

Water is lunar on these solar afternoons;
it is our feelings
always seeking an outlet
always wanting to be heard.

But when it suddenly escapes
the forbidden sanctuary of our inner world
it only leaves behind
these rusty brown stains
on the ceilings and floors.

TRANSUBSTANTIATION

First day of December
bright with newly-fallen snow.

You may have a mouthful of ashes today.

Drink strong coffee
put on your snow tires.

And just remember
that your cold, chapped hands
your incomplete tasks
could still be a stained-glass window.

There could still be someone alive and well
out there
waiting to be resurrected
under the drifting snow.

A HEALING IN EARLY SPRING

The March sun
is grapeseed oil
that refines and loosens the gritty snowbanks.

A holy well beginning to thaw.

The strong gales are mandrake root—
they shriek at first
but then yield comfort food for new growth.

It is a happy, barking dog
that frantically greets you
or a cat perched quietly in a mission lamplit windowsill.

And in your dream
you may see a pretty World War One nurse
offering you healing balm, bandages,
kind words
and a metal cup of rum.

A DREAM ABOUT ROBERT BLY

I mailed the old master
my modest first book of poems
knowing full well
it would never actually reach him.

But in the dream he shambled aboard
the greyhound bus
large, real, somewhat windblown
at a little backwater station.

He took a seat beside me
shuffling to accommodate his bulk
smiling a childlike, shamanic grin

and said:

"You already knew my answer.
It is an empty hand
a temporary journey with strangers
through a field full of snow."

FOXGLOVE

A tattooed young woman
strides past with a year's supply of cat food
and a big bottle of Chilean wine.

An emaciated man
sings in a quavering cigarette-ash voice.
He strums and clunks away on a very old guitar

his open case revealing a few sympathy coins.

For some reason I think
a fist is just an open hand gone bad
and foxglove is only deadly
when it is digitalis.

IF

If you believe in ghosts
you will often see them;
If you believe in astrology
it will truly work;
If you believe in Jesus
he will always be at your side;
If you believe in pyramid power
your house will feel refreshed and vitalized
by their keen presence.

Why is all this white magic so?

Perhaps it's only a road sign
a detour
that points to a receptive
even playful universe.

A SPIRITUAL NIGHTMARE (IN FOUR PARTS)

Well-dressed Jehovah's Witnesses
have come to your door to tell you
that the World Series has been cancelled
due to the coming apocalyptic rapture.
They leave their pamphlet, bless you,
and walk away.

God, it turns out, is William Shatner.

Nothing you've done
has ever made any real difference.

Death is merely oblivion.

A POEM WRITTEN ON BLOOMSDAY

In my dream
God had become tired of life.
Everything had become too predictable
too worthless.
Everything was made in China.

So he called in sick
left for the afternoon
turned off his pager.

He had a few stiff drinks
and hit a bucket of balls
with one of his old ne'er do well buddies.

But the balls were planets and stars
so everything became a cosmic mess
of dust.

Nevertheless, the game was just beginning
once again.

A PRAYER FOR STRESS

Give us this rainy morning
our Eucharist of stress.

Accept it on the tongue
and swallow.

Transforming stress,
healing stress.

Amen.

HANGING ON

What is God?

Some kind of electrical activity?
No answer. Static. No answer.

We rise regardless
check our messages
dutifully water lawns and gardens
check our bank balances.

Some people might even say a little prayer before their morning
coffee.
For themselves or others, or God.

But God doesn't like poems.
Hates them, really.
They are too much like circles
remind him too much of himself.
He threw a lightning bolt at this one.
A direct hit.

And yet what happens
after all this noise?

We don't know
but we hang on tenaciously
to the scrub brush and spiky succulents
that cling to the precipice of eternity.

INITIATION

It's no joke.

Someday the burly, crazy-eyed shaman
is going to pick you
and let out a loud, drunken, frightening hoot
to announce it.

He'll grab you like a rag-doll
take you blindfolded
to the belly of the whale
to the bright operating theatre
where you will die under anesthetic
and watch yourself being re-born by C-section.

He will take you to underground caves
filled with primitive animal paintings
that can be glimpsed dimly by torchlight.

He will make you piss
into the cold December wind.
He'll cut your arm (badly)
and bring you down
to the subway platform at 3 a.m.

You can smell his rum breath
as he shambles toward you
dancing you naked

to a bonfire
in the full-moon winter woods.

GOD'S FACE

Is a full peony
in early June.

A baby sleeping
in an outdoor crib
vulnerable

and omnipotent.

A FINCH SINGING ON A RAINY APRIL MORNING

A melodious, mournful fragment.

Three bright, promising tones
followed by their shadow:
three minor notes—
the last one very sad
mysterious as a human life.

All of art, all of music
must defer to this early, grey wisdom.

PREPARING INDIAN FOOD, JANUARY 2012

Old calendars run out of time.

Outside, snow tires spin on a sheet of black ice.
A harsh, futile sound.

Balder is dying once again—
turning to white ash
in the tall snowbanks.

What else is there to do
when wheels spin and calendars run out?

Ouroboros has eaten everything.
Swallows a candle flame
music, prayers, poems.

Yet some angel still presides
over the cilantro
turmeric
sprig of mint.

Deep cold outside.

Inside, the incense of toasting cardamom seed
touches everything
alive.

HEADSTONES

They abide silent, stoic
through all this noise
all this change.

These letters and numbers
soberly etched in marble
cannot see anyone.

Perhaps someone has been kind enough
to drop a flower
or light a candle here.

Or perhaps not.

Yet even a fleeting thought of this lonely place
this eternal vigil

is like holding a seashell
to the ear.

ABOUT THE MAN

There is a wounded man
limping into deep summer woods

harassed by deerflies and mosquitoes.

The crows witness his frantic progress
and caw encouragingly;
raccoons stare in curiosity.

He seeks the hermit
the healer
who knows the way

to apply the juices of reclusive orchids
frond of fern
claw of crayfish from the clear stream—
a cooling poultice of new life.

He seeks the one who knows how to resurrect the past
through rocks, trees, birdsong,
and simple words.

We all know this wounded man.

He was our father, our mentor,
an anonymous savior in a blizzard, perhaps.

He is inside us always
so we must hope in the end

he makes it.

FAMILY TREE

It was around Halloween—
our young maple still clinging
to its ochre goodbye—
when the would-be family historian

paid us a chatty visit.

His briefcase teeming with spreadsheets, anecdotes,
faces, dates.

He lays out austere, grumpy old photos
of our forefathers
who frown at us from the coffee table—

no nonsense, stoical, dour.

He leaves after pumpkin pie, a mug of Earl Grey
and a few smug, pointed pronouncements
about souls who had departed
many years before his own birth.

"The good is oft interred with their bones".

Later on, by the window
I can almost glimpse a host

of Calvinist shades
still looking for labour

stubbornly refusing to howl in the bitter wind.

A HOT SPELL IN MID-SEPTEMBER

It is unseasonably warm, humid
and it feels like a kind of slow poison
has been touching everything.

The clumsy bees
suffer from progressive dementia
as they absently browse
the ragged, defeated remnants of coneflowers.

Road construction
has spread everywhere
and blocks main arteries.

There are vital secrets returning again to seed
and nature's pain is brewing and fermenting
in roadside gullies.

WHAT HAPPENED?

I'm driving to work in a mist.

Two men stand by the roadside
in the October drizzle
surveying their cars' twisted fenders
wearing that hapless, bemused expression
beyond anger, beyond blame, beyond apology.
Trees shed leaves in the wind
and last night my daughter wriggled out another baby tooth.
Pumpkins have been dutifully placed
on thresholds
and everything is speaking of time.

Is God imperfect like all this?
Was that inscrutable being just sleeping
in some void
until they had that fateful dream
of divinity and evil
and many other inconsequential things?
Perhaps it was then that time began
of its own volition
moving and moving. Never going back.

I think of the two men by the roadside:
it just happened.

SMASHED PUMPKIN

All Saint's Day.

The profane ritual
has been performed again.
Someone hoofed it
like a football
fracturing its obscene grin
spilling its orange, stringy innards
across a very busy road.

Now it has become desecrated sweetbreads
served very cold.

It is a gritty, unholy feast—
a siren call to black squirrels and large crows
with a death wish.

THE COMPACT UNIVERSE

Everything became
smaller, sleeker
holding more and more data
more and more.

Smaller and smaller
until God's eye
the universe itself
could be easily navigated
with a tiny user-friendly menu
built into a funny little phone.

Until God finally answered one day
and everything
past, present, future

exploded

into countless swirling fragments.

And everything started again.

SNOW FORMS (for R. Murray Schafer)

The Inuit, some claim, have a hundred different words for it.

I have no such lexicon.

But I do know
that there is snow that banks very high
in late February
making even young children
understand something of beginnings, endings.

There is the snow that only an owl can see
perched in a high tree branch.

Snow that dissolves, drifts, dances
like a dervish
making contact with another world.

There is the sad, nostalgic type
that falls over everything in "The Dead".

A cave of snow
for a hermit with a lantern.
Solitude snow.

Snow that flies in a wailing wind
banshee-like.

Snow mixed with ice pellets
lashing the faces of people waiting stoically at the bus stop.
The hard grainy kind
that quickly turns to ice
at the end of the driveway.

Or, like this morning, a very light snow
twirling like a forgotten cosmology
a million tiny reasons
melting as they touch the windshield.

A POEM WRITTEN AFTER SHOVELING SNOW

Muttering to myself
about the likely imminence of the plough
about the waste of all this labour.

A neighbour's cat has come to watch me.

It gazes— green saucer-eyed— with that
stunned "I knew you in another lifetime"
look of recognition
that some cats seem to have sometimes.

For some odd reason I think:
wars begin because men are sad
finding anger far more acceptable than tears

especially when they are muttering alone
shoveling
against the inevitable victory of snow.

NEAR CHRISTMAS

I awake early
to the sound of my daughter
laughing in her sleep.

The day is very cold.

Later, the body dreams
of December angels roosting briefly in the temporal world.

Coloured lights are strung haphazardly
over an evergreen.
A few old, forgotten letters are discovered
in a box
while carefully, reverently unpacking
the shiny ornaments
like Mithraic symbols
or Holst's magnificent planets
wrapped in newsprint.

And while the icy wind cuts through the street
in the kitchen
there is curry on toast.

THE FLU

When it's very bad
these painful, gushing convulsions

feel like the body's attempt
to throw off all of human history.
A microcosmic exorcism
at 4 a.m.

But there are more gentle things too
after the body's tectonic plates
have quieted down—

the memory of a January night
years ago.

A father's sympathetic tones
offering a glass of coke or ginger ale
and my brother-in-law venturing out
in his old, unreliable car
to buy me a Captain America comic book

on the coldest evening of the year.

A JOURNEY TO THE MOUNTAINS

In the strange dream
Leonard Cohen had to be located
at some remote mountain monastery
for some reason or other.

Our small search party
started out on snowshoes.

It snowed heavily for six days.
The wind rose and it drifted like an ocean.
Who could find anyone in all this white?

But we finally reached a pavilion-like tent;
a campfire crackling sparks into the air;
prayer flags surrounding the perimeter.

Some experienced guides wearing sheepskin
agreed to lead us up the craggy, treacherous path
to the hermit's cave.

Finally there we were and there he was:
gaunt, haggard, introspective.

We listened with bated breath
waiting for him to speak.

He looked up lugubriously
and muttered something
about wanting stronger, thicker espresso
a more lively female companion
and a high-definition TV.

GAME SEVEN (for Tom Henighan)

A Jungian analyst once said
that the ballpark diamond
is really the quaternity of the mandala—

another modern myth.

How right, I think,
as I watch the bloop single
a two run double
a sacrifice fly.

The crowd erupts in Bacchic frenzy
as one bench moves ecstatic
like the children of Helios
preparing to spray each other with champagne
in the locker room.

While the opposing bench broods, reflects,
and stares
with the somber, contemplative aspect
of Persephone embarking on her yearly voyage

into the dark.

INTROVERT'S SONG

So often it is
when I am alone
walking beneath a waning moon
in the keen air of early spring
that I am most fully
and completely

with others.

LATRINALIA

It sounds like an old Roman festival
but really it's just the kind of
ritualistic scrawl
graffito
that appears in ancient cave paintings
or in that box-like shrine
where public defecation happens.

A mystery cult of purgation.

It could be a few unkind words
scribbled beside a phone number
or some lurid Bacchanal-style drawing
of a huge engorged penis

with a jeering smile
crudely drawn on its priapic head.

A MONASTERY GARDEN

Not only a magnet
for butterflies, hummingbirds—
but for fauns, elves, angels:

these slender purple and white columbines
glowing bee balm
grey-headed coneflower.

Air signs and earth spirits
emerge unexpectedly
like rabbits
from behind stones, smoke bush

revealing themselves only
to the hardworking devout one
whose head is bowed

in deep, prayerful meditation

at dusk.

KINGFISHER

Beautifully oblivious
to a human world of ambition, achievement
and pain
the kingfisher arcs triumphantly
toward moving waters.

WATCHING AN ITALIAN BARBER

He has been in this spot forever—
cut my fuller head of hair when I was just a boy
obsessed with comic book heroes.

White-haired and dignified
he still chews gum and steals furtive glimpses at the World Cup
match
as he diligently works.

He gently tilts the customer's head with a sculptor's knowing hands
squinting, scrutinizing his work in progress
never quite perfectly satisfied
with the length of the sideburn
the maddening cowlick.

He sprays water
judicially snipping, finessing.

And finally, when he is satisfied that the refreshed soul has emerged
he lowers the chair
dusts off the feathery traces of yesterday

and lifts the mirror toward his unsigned portrait.

POEM AT MEECH LAKE

Thought I saw all of Jung's writings
in the veins
of an amber-coloured maple-leaf

found along the steep trail.

CHEETA SPEAKS (1932–)

Hardly anyone knows I'm still around.
The few who do, find it a bit scary.

I don't want to end up a footnote,
a trivia question,
a curio piece on MSN homepages
like Darwin's turtle.

This is the curse of the venerable primate.

But, you know, I've worked
with the best of them;
seen the players come and go.

Back in my studio days
they offered me fine Cuban cigars
and scotch on the rocks at the noisy cast parties.
Gorgeous women doted on me.

Yet now, these halcyon days are quiet, austere.
A high fiber diet; old photographs.

I dabble with oils and acrylics
when I'm up to it
and sleep most of the time.

Pain, depression, frustration—
sure, I've known these in days gone by.

I recall times when they took away the beads
I was frigging with
and I flew into hysterical tantrums.
Or times when they cruelly offered sweets
only to withdraw them.
I justifiably went ballistic.

At least I'm not so bound up by the superego.
Never afraid to let it all hang out.

So why not drop me a line?
I'm still alive...

THE WAREHOUSE

Is vast
bigger than many football fields—
its inventory beyond all reckoning.

Contains vestiges of the late Roman Empire
the U.S. economy
fabulous Chagall stained-glass
missing unicorn tapestries
illuminated texts
and purloined treasures from Europe.

It also houses some dusty old photocopiers
a few electric typewriters
binders of closed contracts
paid invoices.

Some flying buttresses
can be found in the East Wing
as well as a few lipstick-smeared cigarette butts
some oily rags
and a printing press.

A gang of teenagers held a rave here once
and (rumour has it) a group of would-be pagans
performed some ritual or other
on Groundhog Day—
"Imbolc" they called it.

The roof leaks
and it's bitter cold in winter
in spite of an army of space heaters.

The commissionaire is very old
reads political thrillers
and snores his way to a small pension
as he studiously ignores
this sprawling, flyblown
Akashic record.

THE GOBLIN

It was late October—
stark metaphors were scattered everywhere:
a squirrel with half its tail chewed off
a smashed pumpkin by the curb.

And today I met a small, venomous little man
who resembled a goblin.

He had burned out eyes
that had seen too much life—
now gone cold as an unheated cabin
in midwinter woods.

He had a scar on his forehead
that resembled a star
and every word he spoke
was like a mouthful of rusty bolts.

I remember now that it was he who first told me
about the planes crashing on September 11th.

THE PATH

Wander toward a summer forest
frantic with birdsong.
There is a green and shadowy path
you must take

sooner or later.

But first you must make a long list
put aside your worldly goods and ambitions
say goodbye to those you love.

The flashing yellow streak
of canaries
whisking from treetop to treetop
may reassure you that this is the right way.

The cicada's droning mantra
tells you it's alright to go
to disappear and dissolve again.

But make no mistake—
this is still a sad and frightening path.

THE ROAD OF THE MYSTIC

Is very particular—

like the singing grain of a well-used oak floor
that has borne the weight
of many running children
and watched them grow.

Is humble, encouraging
like reading the Whitsun Weddings
or the poems of ecstatic Sufi masters
over morning coffee.

Like seeing the first robin in March
or hearing Horowitz play for the first time.

LINES AT A JAPANESE AUTO REPAIR SHOP

I am greeted at the counter
by a tankful of big festive koi
who seem to proclaim:

"Courage, spirit! Forget about the coming bill."

And then the sagacious, seasoned owner—
whose command of English is halting—
emerges with an explanation of the invoice.

I sense that he has apprehended
some mystical thing
the gross and subtle body of the engine
well-oiled parts moving in unison.

He has understood something very specific
even cruel at times.

He is the high lama
whose sad, sardonic smile
has made the connection
between seized up, cracked parts
and the many blockages
to our bodies and minds

to our human day.

A LESSON

I was very young.
It was my first real classroom—
a night school summer job
filled with mature, worldly-wise students
from here and there.
Trying so hard to find something of value
to give them
struggling— not too successfully— to find
some yet untapped reservoir of wisdom.

Very suddenly
a luna moth sailed in through an open window
like a bird
huge and shamanic.
A few laughed
others were slightly alarmed
by the strange, exotic visitation.

But it was an older student
lately come from Ethiopia
who stared in fascination
with an almost nostalgic look
as though he were staring at glowing coals.
He cupped and cradled the creature
in strong, sturdy, gentle hands
and finally released it
returning it like a goddess
into the sweet, humid night air.

EVENING IN LATE MAY

The sunset burns itself pure
down to the colour of dahlias.

And, to celebrate, we have bought a flat of impatiens—
tenacious yet delicate little flowers—
modest, spartan
little rentals

like our first apartment.

DIVERTIMENTO

A white peony opens in early June.

This morning a centipede
scuttled out from underneath
a damp towel on the hardwood floor

and the hood of my blue car
had been newly-baptized with pollen
from an overhanging tree.

Little fragments of sympathetic magic
are everywhere.

And now I stand in a brand new shirt
middle-aged at the driving range
taking a momentous fresh-air swing.

The ball still resting stoically on its tee
seems to ask
is this the sound of one hand clapping?

ADAM'S PROFESSION

You came to fix the plumbing:
a convenient pretext for an exorcism.

You stick the 30-foot rotating snake
into the bowels of the masonry—
unclogging, probing
helping water to find its urgent path.

You root out all the poisons, blockages
brewing in the old pipes
catch them in an old basin
and dump them out into the back garden
to nourish hollyhocks.

And so, once again, the flotsam
of our everyday lives
has become the modeling clay
of sacred stories.

II   DETOURS

A BIRTHDAY POEM

It is your own day again.

A happy, brief transit of the heart
that must, inevitably, slip through your fingers
like sand
and vanish at dusk
like the neighbor's cat
into the garden.

Every year you must try again
to catch it, pin it down
like a dazzling butterfly
an oriental kite
or some elusive Proteus
that might finally yield

a solar vein of gold.

But once again
it has already passed you
mutely rendered its stoic, numerical declaration
and moved on.

MY PARENTS' COLD STORAGE IN 1972

At first, musty, ripe aromas
and the shadows of masonry jars
housing last year's pickles and chili sauce.
A few cobwebs and a spider in the corner.

A quick tug on a pull cord
and a bare sixty-watt bulb
reveals a basket of potatoes sprouting long eyes
like Gorgon's hair.
Countless Green Giants
arranged on crude shelves
quietly biding their time in the dim coolness.
A bottle of tonic water
stowed away in a box from New Year's
bearing the image of a heavily-bearded, turbaned Indian man
perhaps dreaming of gin from the British Raj.
A few stubby candles, Redbird matches
and a dead field mouse
on the rough concrete floor.

This cool, musty place
is now a faraway, exotic land.

FOLK ART MORNING

March sunlight streaming onto hardwood.

The day is a Spartan
hand-carved masterpiece
rendered sure-handedly
in slightly garish spring colours:
home-spun carnival faces
weatherbeaten textures.

Bacon splatters, sputters in the kitchen
creating its maple incense
beside a long list of errands
clipped onto the fridge
with a beetle-shaped magnet.

A day whose only burdens (so far)
are a wicker basket
of deep green granny smiths
or a donkey grazing in textile landscape
beneath a smiling tin sun from Mexico.

Today is a small child's rocking chair
ornamented with a pair of soulful rainbow trout
swimming vibrant
in two directions.

The child is laughing.
A tiny red-wing blackbird
is glowing on the shelf.

And a green man keeps vigil
over the very first tulip
as it emerges
delicate, vulnerable

into the world's cold, hard glory.

A SÉANCE

Surely it must be more
than some dusty Victorian table rapping
parlor trick automatic writing
lamps flickering right on cue.

And perhaps poetry is the closest thing
we have left to these late night gatherings
in neatly arranged sitting rooms
with doilies, ferns, and silver candlesticks
with handsome mantle clocks soberly ticking.

A poem, after all, still borders
on the spirit world
though it may just as easily succumb
to hoax or sleight of hand.

Would it do any harm, I wonder,—
even in a digital age—
to put on our finest clothes
and jewelry
hold hands in a circle
and be quiet for a moment when it is read?

PHOTOGRAPH

I look at an old photo
taken on a beach somewhere
and I suddenly realize this is not the same world

I have been walking in today.

It was a marginally newer, more naïve planet.

The sky and water were different.

People held their bodies differently—
looked more complacent in their sunglasses.

The sand was whiter, more gritty—
even those picnic sandwiches must have tasted different:
sweeter and more fatty, perhaps.

They say the body renews itself like this
every so often.

These distant images
are the story rings inside a tree.

A CONTRACTOR AT MICHAELMAS

He will show up very early
on a crisp, late September morning.

The trees have yielded to orange and ochre.

You will hear ladders, spades, and tools
clattering around in his old pick-up
while you wipe the sleep from your eyes.

He has no time for sophistry or small talk.
Only time to begin.

He will dig deep
excavate your foundations
right down to their footings.

He is a rough poem
trying urgently to heal

guiding Persephone back into the thirsty earth
with a weeping tile.

THE YARD SALE

God is having a yard sale.
He's finally moving.

Everything is spread out
haphazardly on an endless lawn
while a chamber music quartet
plays the cheerful strains of Mozart.

But it's really just the usual stuff:

A few worn out rag dolls
the vestiges of one or two empires
the contents of a cosmic safety deposit box
a few icons of immortality
a bag of stardust
one dwarf star.

And, of course, an old dog-eared yearbook
with a few absurd things written in it.

AUTUMN COCKTAIL

There is no set recipe.
No courses you can take.

You gradually learn how
to make it over time.

1 part melancholia
3 parts sex
2 parts fear.

Add puree of pumpkin to taste
a dash of Tabasco
2 scoops of ice.

Mix 2 healthy jiggers of vermouth, tonic, and bitters.

Shake well.

Finish with a twist of fate
and a healthy splash of mortality.

FARM FOR SALE (SOUTHERN ONTARIO)

Something reveals itself
briefly, shyly
at the old white farmhouse
embraced by wide green summer country.

Something in its modest sunroom
its gables protected
by four protestant lightning rods.

A barn that once teemed with cats
now only houses oily John Deere tractors
sitting idle like museum pieces.

A barking dog is still the only doorbell.

There is something about the long, slow summers of childhood
nearing harvest time
and a farmer's convincing story
of a UFO seen in the deep country darkness
told in the stoic measured, tones
of a sure-handed, sensible man
who had been a World War Two aviator.

The tall trees spread out over the dusty lane.

A place where life has flourished
and ashes rest.

SPRING

An unmistakable season.
Like biting into a clove.

Pot-bellied motorcycle riders
are its first herald
thundering up the late-March afternoon.

Then the old retired men, suburban patricians,
come out of hibernation
to stoically assess the condition
of their muddy, mushy lawns
nowhere near ready for raking.

Last is the young woman
on the downtown corner—
a street-seasoned Persephone—
in shiny leather jacket and boots
burning passing cars
with her defiant stare
pushing her way out of the underworld

like a half-frozen tulip.

POEM ON GOOD FRIDAY

An awakening, groggy earth
nurses its ice-wine hangover.

Its heart begins to speak in rivers and streams.

Craters and potholes have widened;
bleached, resurrected scraps of paper
fly like liberated avatars in the wind.

It's no wonder the Celts fell in love
with the Christian story
with all its rocks and thorns.

In the tawny grass
a few impossibly yellow and lilac crocuses
are splashing like sacred animation.

Raking must be done.
Taxes must be paid.
The tomb must be found
empty
so the swollen rivers can flow
and the robin can nest in the eaves.

SPRING RAKING

It is very light work—
more like sweeping.

Extricating a few gnarled leaves
from around the cedar hedge
scratching up some twigs
and clumps of dead, yellow grass.

But there are a few surprises, at least:
a green plastic soldier
well-camouflaged in the mud
a child's charm bracelet
a bleached fragment
of a once-ominous headline.

Later that evening
I drive through the neighbourhood
on an errand

discover a very old limestone convent

that I'd never even noticed before.

SIGNS

A very welcome visitor
to the old claw-foot tub.

A fellow-struggler
this tiny spider
who crawls— determined as an Alexander—

over the shower curtain
amid a cascade that must be like a Niagara.

Yet another reason to push on with it.

NIGHT DRIVE, PRINCE EDWARD COUNTY

Deep country dark.

The half moon steals furtive glimpses
from behind drifting cloud.

Something reddish darts
across the county road—
a fox?

The fluttering moths that perform
their temporary dance
in the high beams
say you are alone in all this.

Thought I saw Al Purdy's ghost
shambling along the shoulder of the road
into a reedy thicket.

STORIES IN LATE OCTOBER

Heavy rain this morning.

The fallen maple leaves resemble
ancient frescoes from Pompeii
and the few flowers that remain
appear funereal now
solemnly awaiting the last word of frost.

It is time to look at all our stories once again
now that their roots and bones are showing through.

Time to reflect upon chance encounters
that promised much
but often led to puzzling cul de sacs.

Why do these stark, maddening loose ends
always flap like a scarecrow's hat
in the cold wind

forbidding any real interpretation?

TWO MOMENTS IN WINTER

I

The lacy shadows of the sumac's branches
in the winter moonlight
spread out delicately across the new snow
like a nervously-executed line drawing.

II

An austere moment of balance
as the red winter sun sets
and the winter moon rises full
over a dusky rose skyline.

THE USES OF A COLD

My body is snowbound
with heavy phlegm
the head is groggy, dreamy

and nothing seems so linear now.

And so it is time
to listen to the body once again
and truly hear its hidden needs, pains, doubts.

Time to go back to its reservoir of past memories
embedded so deep in bones and tissue.

Time to be patient
like an icicle slowly dripping.

MANTRA IN LATE SEPTEMBER

The first killing frost

touches everything like some drunken Midas
as it will touch us eventually—
mellowing our flames to softly glowing embers
returning our carefully-tended perennials
to stalky oblivion.

Last night I dreamed
that the "boys from the hood"—
swaggering with baggy-pant bravado
and oversized sports jerseys—
had talked to Jung by an autumn lake
in the Gatineau hills.

He listened, laughed, and understood
their anger.
And their hearts
were suddenly touched by Christ.

Then sad gentle smiles played over
their hard-bitten faces
as they began the deep guttural droning chant
of Tibetan monks.

SONG FOR THE OVERPASS

The blunt concrete overpass
swelters in mid-July haze.

At the stoplight
amid cigarette butts and discarded coffee cups
I see the raggedy weeds
that have pushed their way into life
through cracks in the hot cement.

Slightly obscene versions
of their tame garden cousins
they grow wild and funky
like guitar-toting street kids
sporting piercings and tattoos.

They grow scruffy and spread
like a feral cat colony
at an abandoned industrial site.

Someone should light a stick of incense
to remember the misbegotten want-to-be's
who grow wild and neglected
through cement and asphalt.

REMEDY FOR A HANGOVER

The ancient Romans
recommended five owl's eggs—
taken raw.

But one should also try

a plate of Spanish rice
a glass of whole milk
a leisurely stroll past a statue or two.

THE MAN WHO HAS ALWAYS BEEN AT THE CORNER

I know this man.

I see him each morning
in a variety of bland disguises.

His face is stark
unrelenting as a concrete pillar
or a curb.
It is a page of tiny stock-market figures
transformed into a cynical jeer.

He is a leather briefcase
full of forbidding documents.

He has put deadbolts and padlocks
on his rose garden.
His hydrangeas are too big—
almost a threat.

He knows the esoteric language of by-laws
fence height regulations, and other irritating minutiae.

His calico cat shits in my daughter's sandbox
as he dutifully drains his swimming pool
into the lotus blossom of the mind.

He suffers nightmares about moonlight,
the forest, the ocean
but tells no one about it.

He was always there
when I was a child running fast
—and supposedly free—
through summer fields.

A FEW LINES IN JUNE

The day is sprinkled
with spicy, commonplace metaphors:
a feisty red-winged blackbird
chases off a huge madly-flapping crow
near the roadside strawberry stand.

BY THE ROAD

Chicory and Queen Anne's lace
igniting blue and white
in the ditch.

Bindweed and trumpet vine
usurping the old fence.

This is the ragged
exotic garden
of some resident wind god.

COYOTES (CALGARY, LATE AUGUST)

A very open place
where a freight train is not only heard
but fully seen
and felt
mournful, deep and inevitable
within the changing, imperfect body.

And yet they always know its coming
before we do.

They exult like frenzied children
in the night air;
herald the lonely horn
with a high-pitched chorus
of yips and howls

as an impossibly huge
harvest moon
rises orangey-red
over the hills.

FEEDING CHICKADEES MIDWINTER

Well-versed in the sobriety of snow
that clings to the spreading branches
they pulse down
very suddenly
to our still, outstretched palms.
They light for an eternal flash
like tiny spirits
snatch up a sunflower seed
and thrum instantly back
to the safety of evergreens.
Even here there are many shadows
yet a poem remains
an open, vulnerable hand

making its imperfect offering to the light.

SAMSARA

Had gone to the Quebec countryside
to learn how to cross-country ski
with a seasoned trail guide named Pierre.

One moment I was gliding
like an unfettered astral being
through the fresh white woods

then suddenly flat on my ass
tangled up in the scratchy trees
legs akimbo
while the chickadees laugh.

But it was lovely; worth every bruise.
My eight year-old daughter raced ahead of me
without any poles.

Later that evening, I was reading a book
on Tibetan Buddhism.
It declared that all this is maya, illusion
leading to pain, suffering
possible rebirth in lower realms.

Let go of all this it said.
All this transient love, sickness, jostling,
desire, death, and inconvenience.
Be enlightened. Free of the hungry ghosts.

This is one way to see it.

Or is this better, I wonder,
as I try awkwardly to stand up again
bruised, cold, and stiff on the mid-winter trail.

The chickadees are quiet now
and my daughter is already
far off ahead of me
in the distance.

SNOW ANGELS

The child is a conjurer.

She laughingly summons invisible, inarticulate seraphim
to this pure, blank sheet
of January snow.

PRAYER ON ALL SAINTS' DAY

Time to venerate the fallen leaves
desecrate the Jack o' Lantern.

Time to switch to heavy jackets
and tuck cold hands deep
into the linty underworld of overcoat pockets
where you may discover an old list
of last year's errands.

A few still not done.

ST. FRANCIS BURIED IN SNOW

The year's first snowfall
is thick, slushy.
Our small statue
capped now with a white peak
is brooding in the long-spent garden.
A black squirrel
ranges wildly over the hydro lines
berserk with newly-ignited energy
jumps suddenly onto a heavy white tree branch
and knocks loose a wet clump of snow
that plummets hard to the ground—
inevitable as another day of work.
A blessing of sorts.

STAR OF BETHLEHEM

There is a snow-covered billboard
gaudily announcing some outdoor
nativity pageant
at this, the rawest time of the year.

Nearby, a flock of sparrows chase off a crow.

I am reminded, as always, of all this daily vulnerability
in spite of the fact we usually come through it—
though somewhat scarred, nonplussed,
broken in a few places.

And this is why
we lift the mug of rum and eggnog
a rich, nutmeg-flavoured salute
to steady us for that cold, inevitable reality

of a winter birth.

MOONLIGHT

I rise in the middle of the night
after a strange dream of the past.

Soft, spectral light caresses the oak floor
beside the staircase.

YOU STILL NEED A POEM BECAUSE

It is a pleasantly pyrrhic victory
an essential anachronism
accomplishing nothing
but deep transformation.

It is childlike enough to notice
a half-moon rising
over the tattooed drifter
resting under an oak tree near the fairgrounds.

It is a lantern in a very deep forest.

It is a suspicious package
seriously rattling those who are afraid to open it.

And it is also a plume of white smoke
heralding the birth of a newly-minted angel

or a venerable pope.

CATERPILLAR'S SONG

Chewing up the leaves
of another day
watching a trapped hornet
buzzing in the windowsill.

Hoping for change.
Fearing it too.

EARLY FLOWERS

I admire the tenacity
of these papery, vulnerable
splashes of yellow and purple
erupting into the chilly April air.

They are like the young woman I saw
with an umbrella and dancer's legs
walking purposefully

into the cold, driving rain.

SYMBIOSIS

The weird ones
the mavericks
desperately need the conventional, sober ones
to define the corners of their own universe
would, in fact, be nothing
without their conservative counterparts.
And vice versa, I suppose.

I will wrap this small truth up in newspaper
and bring it to the agora.

ROAD TRIP

It is midsummer.

We travel down an unfamiliar highway—

past discarded bottles on the shoulder
and several variations on the road-kill theme

past Queen Anne's lace and devil's paintbrush
asserting their brief life in the ditch
past french fry stands
and crudely lettered "blackberries for sale" signs.

We come to a turn off
near the big flat rocks
where some bored travelers inscribed
their initials.

It is a junction
that hadn't been marked on the map.
The GPS has no record of it.

Twenty kilometers of winding dirt road
flanked by deep, deep woods.
Very bumpy—
our tires hurling little pebbles everywhere.

A jack rabbit darts in front of us—
narrowly missed him.
Then the wild, funky stench of skunk.

We reach the lake as darkness falls.
A full moon rises.

We feel we have been here before
but cannot name the place.
Figures slowly emerge from the pines
congregating around the enormous bonfire—
an assembly grand and disparate
as the cover of Sgt. Pepper's.

They are all shrewd and complete again.

A few dead uncles drink beer
from stubby brown bottles
talking fearlessly about the morning
and long-forgotten pennant races.

Pierre Trudeau is having a friendly, polite chat
with Ava Gardner.

And who is that blue-eyed old man
reading poems beside the fire
as bats flutter zig-zag over the twilight lake?

Fireflies appear
timber wolves wail in the distance

and we are alone again

holding cat-tails and moonlight.

SOME THOUGHTS IN A TENT

After the deep
pitch black of mother night
with no lantern
wolves singing in the distance
and animal sounds all around
dawn is no longer just another
bland, coffee grind day
but a solar goddess of salvation
inviting you
to unzip the superfluous fabric door
and drink the sweet pine-scented air

of morning.

AFTERWORD BY HENRY BEISSEL

Detours, Daniel Boland's second collection of poetry, is the work of a poet in search of ultimate meanings and ultimate encounters. Boland knows that a poet's vision must reach beyond appearances. His poems acknowledge that things are what they seem to be, but they are also gateways to a reality beyond them, just out of reach of the senses and of words that can only be gestures in their direction.

Boland understands that—understands that the language of poetry is image and metaphor, and that they open windows unto a world we cannot know, but which the poem evokes to the inner eye and ear. His voice calls us into the intimacy of a world in which all things interrelate in a complex web of being.

In the 44 poems that constitute Part I ("If") of the collection, the poet confronts us time and again with images that point beyond themselves. A "flight of butterflies" becomes a fluttering of "tiny flags of independence, the "March sun" is "a happy, barking dog... or a cat perched quietly in a mission lamplit windowsill", while " a fist is just an open hand gone bad" and our "cold, chapped hands" challenge them to be "a stained glass window".

Everywhere in these poems transcendental realities seem to urge themselves upon the reader. We catch a glimpse of the elusive face of "God" in a "full peony/in early June", but he or she can't be pinned down. Valiantly, the poet asserts in the title poem of this section that "If you believe" in things, you'll see them, they'll be there; but already in the last stanza he draws back and wonders: "Perhaps it's only a road sign/a detour/that points to a receptive/even playful universe." Appropriately, in the next poem, "God, it turns out, is William Shatner."

While earnest in their quest for the unknowable, these poems also delight the reader with their wit and playfulness. Especially the 39 poems of Part II ("Folk Art Morning") include a wide range of subject matter from the banal to the sublime: a birthday, a séance, a photograph, a contractor, a hangover, the flu, coyotes, samsara, and a caterpillar's song. Nothing escapes Boland's attention, and everything reverberates with the presence of another world:

Birthday is "a happy, brief transit of the heart/that must.../vanish at dusk/like the neighbor's cat/into the garden." A day in March is "a small child's rocking chair/ornamented with a pair of soulful rainbow trout/swimming vibrant/in two directions." Old photographs are "the story rings inside a tree." And as you mix and shake an "Autumn Cocktail" you "finish with a twist of fate/and a healthy splash of mortality."

I find it hard to resist the temptation to go on quoting the many memorable lines in these splendid poems. They invite you to join them on their adventurous quest for what is true in this world of will-o'-the-wisp where "there are many shadows/yet a poem remains/an open, vulnerable hand/ making its imperfect offering to the light." This rich collection of poems rewards many readings, leaving us with a sense of delight and wonderment at our gloriously bewildering world.

Henry Beissel, December 15, 2013

Other Volumes

in the STONE FLOWER PRESS poetry series:

Daniel Boland *Toward the Chrysalis* (2005)

Christopher Levenson *Local Time* (2006)

Robert Powell *Harvest of Light* (2007)

Tom Henighan *Time's Fools* (2010)